Cellar

by Steven Otfinoski

illustrated by
Beth Peck

MODERN CURRICULUM PRESS
Pearson Learning Group

CHARACTERS

NARRATOR   BEN BROWN   TOM WILSON   MR. BROWN

NARRATOR: It is a beautiful Saturday morning. Puffy billows of white clouds fill the blue sky. Ben is coming up the steps from his cellar. Billows of dust come up from the basement with him. He is carrying a pile of old newspapers. His friend Tom walks by. Ben bellows a loud hello.

BEN: Hello, Tom! Where are you going?

TOM: I'm going to play basketball over at Mike's house. Do you want to come along?

BEN: Thanks. But I'm busy.

Tom: It looks as if you're stuck cleaning out your cellar. What a way to spend a Saturday!

Ben: Oh, I'm not cleaning. I'm hunting.

Tom: Hunting for what?

Ben: For treasure!

Tom: Ben, what are you talking about?

Ben: It's a long story.

Tom: Go ahead. I'm listening.

BEN: Well, my Uncle Albert was an explorer. He discovered a tomb in Egypt.

TOM: A tomb with a mummy in it?

BEN: That's right. And there was treasure in the tomb too. Uncle Albert gave most of it to a museum. But Dad says he kept the best thing for himself.

TOM: What is it doing in your cellar?

Ben: When Uncle Albert died, all his things came to our house. We put them in the cellar. My Dad says if I can find the treasure in all his stuff, it's mine.

Tom: Wow! That's great!

Ben: Well, I'd better get back to work. The cellar is loaded with junk. I've got to take it all out to find the treasure.

TOM: Ben, you have a big job ahead of you. Would you like some help?

BEN: But I thought you were going to play basketball.

TOM: Oh, I can play basketball anytime.

BEN: That's a great offer, Tom. But I wouldn't want you to work for nothing.

TOM: Well, what if we split any treasure we find? That would be fair, wouldn't it?

Ben: I guess so. Okay, Tom. If we find the treasure, we'll split it.

Tom: Great! Let's get to work!

Narrator: For two hours, Tom and Ben drag everything out of the cellar. They find old furniture, dusty boxes, and a stuffed bird with tufts of feathers. More dust billows up. They put the worthless things by the curb. They put the other things back in the cellar.

Tom: I don't get it, Ben. We didn't find any treasure, just this picture of a guy. Who do you think he is?

Ben: It's Uncle Albert! Look at those tufts of white hair under his hat!

Tom: Don't tell me this is the treasure?

Ben: Well, it could be. Uncle Albert had a funny sense of humor.

Tom: But you said we'd find real treasure.

Ben: Well, Uncle Albert did like to tell tall tales. Maybe he made up the part about the treasure.

Tom: Or maybe his nephew did! Did you make up this whole treasure story to get me to help you clean your cellar?

NARRATOR: At that moment, Mr. Brown, Ben's dad, bellows a hello from the doorway. Then he comes outside.

MR. BROWN: It looks as if you guys did a great job cleaning!

BEN: Thanks, Dad. I couldn't have done it without Tom.

Mr. Brown: Good for you, Tom. It's nice to see friends helping each other. Here's the ten dollars I promised. Five for each of you.

Narrator: Mr. Brown then hands each boy a five-dollar bill. Tom looks surprised and very pleased.

Tom: Thanks, Mr. Brown!

Mr. Brown: Thank you, Tom. You can put that picture of Uncle Albert out with the other trash. We have much better pictures of him.

Narrator: Mr. Brown goes back inside the house.

Tom: So much for your treasure!

Ben: But you did get five dollars, didn't you?

Tom: That's the part I can't figure out. Why didn't you just tell me your dad would pay me for helping, instead of telling me that crazy treasure story?

BEN: If I had told you, would you have helped me?

NARRATOR: Tom thinks for a moment. Then he bellows out a laugh.

TOM: No, I guess I wouldn't have. It was the treasure that caught my interest. But now I'm glad to have the five dollars.

NARRATOR: The two friends shake hands. Then Ben picks up the picture of Uncle Albert.

Tom: If you don't mind, I'd like that picture.

Ben: What for?

Tom: It just might come in handy when I have to clean out my cellar. I know some other guys who might be interested in going on a "treasure hunt" too.

Narrator: The two friends laugh.

The End